Grand Canyon National Park

Nate Frisch

Published by
CREATIVE EDUCATION

P.O. Box 227, Mankato, Minnesota 56002
Creative Education is an imprint of The Creative Company
www.thecreativecompany.us

Design and production by Danny Nanos of Gilbert & Nanos
Art direction by Rita Marshall
Printed in the United States of America

Photographs by Alamy (Inge Johnsson, National Geographic Image Collection, Tom Till), Corbis, Dreamstime (Dallasphotography), Getty Images (Antenna Audio Inc.), iStockphoto (angelo elefante, eric foltz), Shutterstock (Ammit, Andy Dean Photography, Apaterson, Boris15, Mike Buchheit, Andrew Burns, Cardaf, R Carner, Jim Feliciano, fivespots, Bill Florence, Tom Grundy, Brendan Howard, Ronnie Howard, Daniel Korzeniewski, Mary Lane, Manamana, Caitlin Mirra, Morgan DDL, mundoview, ozoptimist, Pacific Northwest Photography, pashabo, oksana.perkins, James M Phelps Jr, pmphoto, Mike V. Shuman, Kenneth Sponsler, T-Design, Gleb Tarro, Cristophe Testi, Arlene Treiber, kwan tse, Vlad Turchenko, Krzysztof Wiktor, gregg williams)

Library of Congress Cataloging-in-Publication Data

Frisch, Nate.
Grand Canyon National Park / by Nate Frisch.
p. cm. — (Preserving America)
Includes bibliographical references and index.
Summary: An exploration of Grand Canyon National Park, including how its enormous canyon was formed,
its history of preservation, and tourist attractions such as the overlook called Mather Point.

ISBN 978-1-60818-196-4
1. Grand Canyon National Park (Ariz.)—Juvenile literature. I. Title.
F788.F86 2013
979.1'32—dc23   2012023230

FIRST EDITION

2 4 6 8 9 7 5 3 1

Cover & page 3: *Havasu Creek in the Grand Canyon interior; a turkey vulture*

CREATIVE EDUCATION

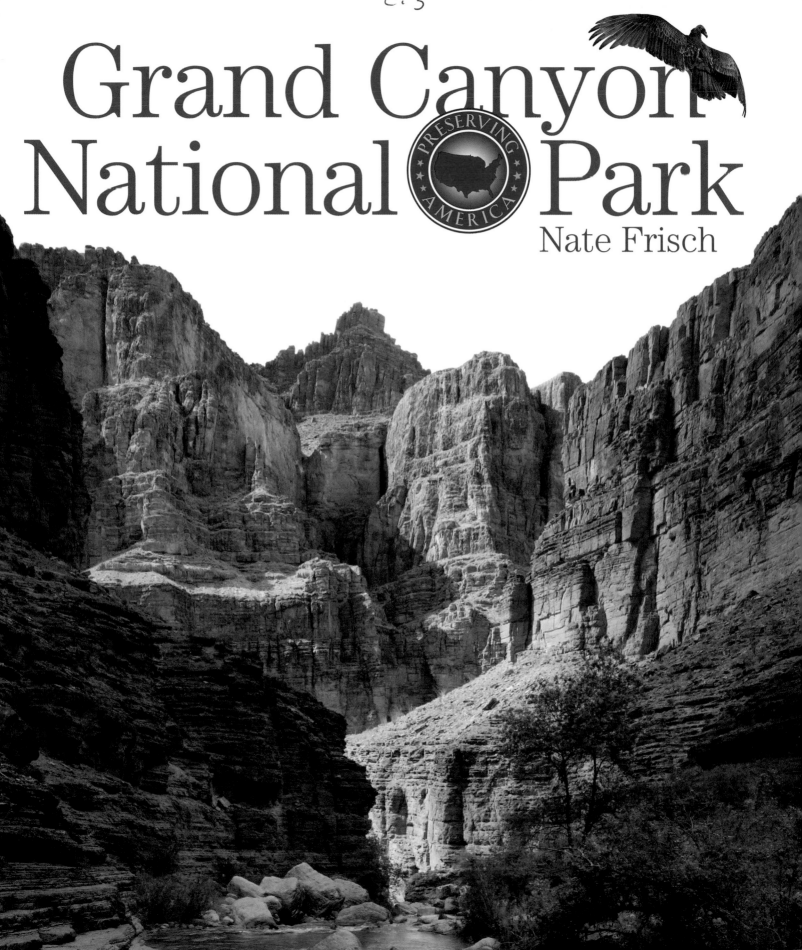

C. 3

Grand Canyon National Park

Nate Frisch

Table of Contents

C. 3

TOWERING MOUNTAINS and glassy lakes. Churning rivers and dense forests. Lush prairies and baking deserts. The open spaces and natural wonders of the United States once seemed as limitless as they were diverse. But as human expansion and development increased in the 1800s, forests and prairies were replaced by settlements and agricultural lands. Waterways were diverted, wildlife was over-hunted, and the earth was scarred by mining. Fortunately, many Americans fought to preserve some of the country's vanishing wilderness. In 1872, Yellowstone National Park was established, becoming the first true national park in the world and paving the way for future preservation efforts. In 1901, Theodore Roosevelt became U.S. president. He once stated, "There can be no greater issue than that of conservation in this country," and during his presidency, Roosevelt signed five national parks into existence. The National Park Service (NPS) was created in 1916 to manage the growing number of U.S. parks—a number that, in 1919, came to include the Grand Canyon. In the nearly 100 years since then, sweeping vistas of the almost impossibly deep canyons of Arizona have made Grand Canyon possibly the most recognized park in the U.S. and an icon of American preservation.

A Landscape Aptly Named

Considered one of the seven natural wonders of the world, the Grand Canyon lives up to its title. While the region contains a collection of varied rock formations that are impressive in their own right and contribute to its grandness, it is the canyon—or rather canyons— that dominate and define the landscape. The main canyon winds for 277 miles (446 km), with a maximum depth of more than a mile (1.6 km) and a maximum width of about 18 miles (29 km). From this central canyon branches a maze of secondary gorges. This enormous labyrinth of stone seems timeless, but it is relatively young. Earth has a history of nearly 4.5 billion years, but it was only about 6 million years ago that the Colorado River and its **tributaries** began shaping the canyons.

While the shaping of land is a relatively new occurrence on Earth, the Colorado **Plateau** Province—the area of land into which the rivers carved—is far more ancient. This huge region covers more than 130,000 square miles (336,700 sq km) and throughout time has experienced different geological movements from surrounding areas. While areas around the plateau have cracked or been disrupted by movements within the earth, the plateau generally remained intact, maintaining a natural record of the planet's history.

The age of the rock around the Grand Canyon varies significantly depending on its depth in the earth, with the deepest layers of stone usually being the oldest. This horizontal, "young-to-old" layering is known as superposition. In the deepest trenches of the Grand Canyon, rock layers thought to be nearly 2 billion years old are visible. Many of

these base layers are made up of igneous and metamorphic rock. Igneous rock is formed from rock that has melted and solidified again, and metamorphic rock is created when previously existing rock is physically changed by extreme heat and pressure. Vishnu Schist, a metamorphic rock, and Zoroaster Granite, an igneous rock, are among the region's ancient rock layers, each formed more than 1.5 billion years ago. What happened during the next billion years is generally unknown, because whatever rock was created has since **eroded**.

Over the course of the past 550 million years or so, the area that is now northern Arizona was, at different periods of time, the site of enormous sand dunes, broad muddy rivers, and shallow tropical seas. A record of each period is now preserved in the form of sedimentary rock, which is made of small sediments compressed together. Over millions of years, dunes became sandstone, mud became shale, and

This photo, taken from an altitude of six miles (10 km), shows the chasms that make up the middle portion of the Grand Canyon

11

Millions of years' worth of erosion brought about by the Colorado River created the extraordinary gorge of the Grand Canyon

seashells became limestone. As many as 40 layers of rock from
10 distinct eras have a combined thickness of more than 5,000 feet
(1,524 m) in some parts of the canyon.

These immensely thick but relatively frail sedimentary layers
were susceptible to drastic erosion, but until about 60 million years ago,
the region where the Grand Canyon now exists was generally flat, with
an elevation near sea level. Any running water in the area likely flowed
slowly, with little force. But then movement within the earth began
raising the Colorado Plateau Province, and by 5 million years ago, the
elevation had increased by as much as a mile (1.6 km). This created two
key ingredients for rapid erosion—water and slopes. The higher altitudes
were cooler, and as moving air rose to pass over the land, moisture in the
air condensed into rain. The rainwater descended swiftly toward lower
ground, creating or bolstering rivers that included the Colorado.

At lower elevations downstream, the climate remained **arid**,
which further enhanced the rivers' effect in shaping the canyons.
The dry land did not absorb water, and there was little plant life to hold
the soil in place. Water rushed across the land, prying loose particles
of sedimentary rock as it went. These particles then drifted with the
current, scraping the earth like sandpaper.

The Colorado River and its tributaries were typically shallow and
broad when they first flowed over the unbroken landscape, but as stone
was worn away, waterways became deeper. The deepest parts of the
river were also the most forceful, and their rapids shaped ever deeper
river bottoms. This trend gradually transformed the rivers from flat
sheets of water to deeper, narrower rapids and explains why the oldest
areas of erosion, at the top of the canyons, are often much wider than
newer erosion at the bottom.

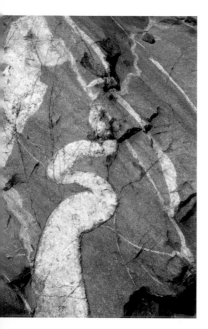

Varying rock layers, including Vishnu Schist (above), and changing light conditions can give the canyon a surprising range of color

The exact shapes of the canyon were determined by varying speeds of erosion. Scientists estimate that the Grand Canyon became an average of 6.5 inches (16.5 cm) deeper every 1,000 years, but the actual rate depended largely on the consistency of the rock layers. Shale is the least resilient of the canyons' sedimentary rocks, while limestone is the most resistant to erosion. Periods of rapid erosion created more gradual slopes, while slower change left sheer cliffs. Because of the many different layers of rock in the Grand Canyon, it is common for a single canyon wall to alternate between straight cliffs and more moderate angles. In many areas of the Grand Canyon, rivers have worn through all the sedimentary layers and reached the much harder Vishnu Schist below. This layer has drastically slowed further shaping of the canyon, which has deepened by only about 500 feet (152 m) in the last 3.8 million years.

Today, the image most commonly associated with the Grand Canyon is that of a magnificent vista overlooking the gaping main canyon, with a maze of smaller gorges breaking up the landscape beyond. Such panoramic views are breathtaking, but the more subtle details, rock formations, and plant and animal life within the region are also remarkable.

From a distance, much of the Grand Canyon appears to be brown or reddish brown in color. In truth, many canyon walls aren't brown—at least not entirely. The walls exhibit the contrasting layers of rock from the past 2 billion years, and these layers may be red, pink, orange, olive

green, blue-gray, or white. When examined up-close, the intricacy of the stone is often surprising. It may be deeply grooved, pitted, or covered by small, irregular nodules that appear too delicate for a region so rugged.

The Grand Canyon is not all arid, bare stone. Many of the rivers that formed the landscape still flow through the canyons and gorges, and numerous waterfalls and rapids still eat away at bits of stone in the river bottoms. Surprisingly lush vegetation grows along many of the waterways, and vines and other plants can be found clinging to sheer cliffs near waterfalls. Ranging from about 1,000 to 9,000 feet (305–2,743 m) in altitude, the Grand Canyon region contains several distinct **ecosystems**, including deserts, scrubland, pine forests, and grassy meadows. These varying habitats are home to more than 1,500 plant species as well as 355 kinds of birds, 89 mammals, 47 reptiles, 17 fish, and 9 amphibians. Plants range from hardy cacti and lichens to leafy ferns and wildflowers. Notable animals include bighorn sheep, mountain lions, black bears, mule deer, elk, California condors, Gila monsters, and rattlesnakes.

The Gila monster is the only venomous lizard found in the United States, but it moves very slowly and poses little threat to people

The Grand Canyon is a unique area in that it does not have just one climate. A high-altitude location in the region may be 40 °F (22 °C) cooler than a spot down within a canyon. Areas at higher altitudes also receive more precipitation, but even they are relatively dry. The area's lack of cloud cover and low humidity allow temperatures to change drastically from day to night, and a daily swing of 30 °F (17 °C) is common. In the winter, precipitation may fall as snow on the upper rims, while the warmer canyons will more likely receive rain.

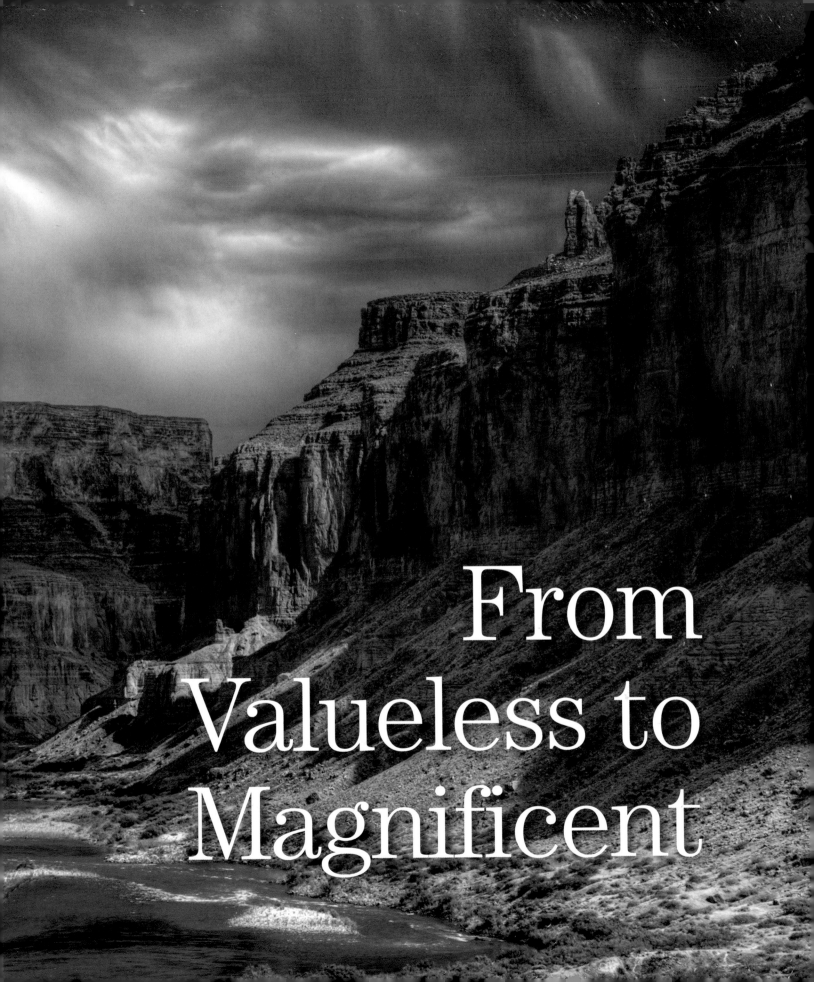

From
Valueless to
Magnificent

The region that today includes Grand Canyon National Park has long been inhabited by humans, and artifacts dating back 12,000 years have been found there. The region's earliest residents were likely small bands of hunter-gatherers who moved across the land following the migrations of the bison, ground sloths, mountain goats, and other large animals they hunted during the **ice age** of the time.

Around 3,000 years ago, people called Ancestral Puebloans living in the canyons began growing crops including corn, beans, and squash. They built permanent villages called pueblos in which homes made of stone or mud bricks were built against one another (and sometimes canyon walls) to form communal structures. Over the centuries, they developed bows and arrows, dug irrigation canals, grew cotton for weaving cloth, and created earthen pottery. Then, for reasons that are still unknown, tribes that had developed this advanced culture seemed to disappear between 700 and 800 years ago. Soon after, other tribes—including the Hopi, Southern Paiute, Havasupai, and Navajo—came to the canyons and followed many of the same ways of life.

The first Europeans to encounter the Grand Canyon were likely Spaniards in the mid-1500s. Armed Spanish explorers called conquistadors had already plundered many riches from the Aztecs in Mexico and were hungry for more wealth. A quest for a mythical city of gold led Francisco Vásquez de Coronado and 300 Spanish soldiers to the Grand Canyon around 1540. Not finding any gold, the Spaniards soon departed, giving little further thought to the incredible landscape upon which they had stumbled.

The Spanish returned in the early 1600s, this time to spread their influence through Christian missionaries. Missions were built near Hopi villages of the eastern Grand Canyon region, but the Hopi resisted these

Pottery made by Indians in the Southwest was often painted in colors that mirror those of the Grand Canyon's environment

attempts to change their beliefs and way of life, and the Indians drove the missionaries out around 1680. A Spanish army returned to the area to force compliance upon the Hopi, but the Indians' knowledge of the winding canyons gave them a decided advantage over the would-be conquerors. Ultimately, the Spaniards decided the desolate region was not worth the effort—a sentiment that was shared by other explorers until the 1800s.

In 1857, the U.S. government ordered an expedition to explore the Colorado River. Led by Army Lieutenant Joseph Ives, a crew of 24 men traversed the river aboard the steamboat *Explorer*. The alternating rough rapids and shallow sandbars frequently delayed and finally ruined

Ancestral Puebloans carved many homes and granaries (food storage rooms) into cliffs, such as these along the Nankoweap Trail

Explorer. Without even having reached the heart of the canyons, Ives stated that the Grand Canyon looked like "the gates of hell" and concluded that the region had little value beyond a scientific point of view.

The Grand Canyon remained mostly unexplored and uncharted by white Americans until 1869, when Major John Wesley Powell—a Civil War veteran and geologist—prepared to lead a voyage that would travel from Green River, Wyoming, to Lake Mead along the Arizona–Nevada border. The journey would follow the Green and Colorado rivers and pass all the way through the Grand Canyon.

The expedition faced hardships from the very beginning. Powell had to personally raise funds for the journey, and the party included just

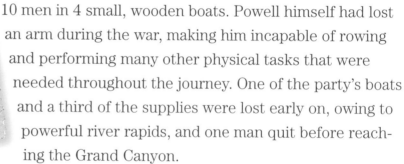

10 men in 4 small, wooden boats. Powell himself had lost an arm during the war, making him incapable of rowing and performing many other physical tasks that were needed throughout the journey. One of the party's boats and a third of the supplies were lost early on, owing to powerful river rapids, and one man quit before reaching the Grand Canyon.

This stamp commemorates the 1869 expedition led by John Wesley Powell that helped introduce the Grand Canyon to the world

The trials within the canyons were even greater. While Powell marveled at the humbling scale of the region, others felt trapped by the sheer cliffs and feared the dangerous rapids and falls of the river. More critically, they were desperately low on supplies and nearly starving. Three of the remaining nine men left the party, planning to backtrack out of the canyon. They were never seen again. During a land survey, Powell's handicap nearly cost him his life while scaling steep cliffs. But after almost a month in the canyons, the explorers emerged safely, having followed the Colorado River the entire way through.

Tales of Powell's journey spread throughout the U.S. and beyond,

piquing interest in an area that had long been ignored or avoided. Other explorers grew eager to investigate the giant canyons for themselves. Powell led another expedition into the Grand Canyon in 1871; this time, his party was better prepared and encountered far fewer problems. This second voyage was more thorough than the first and produced many of the first maps and photographs of the region.

Adventurers and researchers aside, many of the region's first nonnative residents arrived with the completion of railroads just south of the Grand Canyon in the 1880s. These early settlers included gold-seeking miners hoping to strike it rich. Some gold was found, but the amount of time and effort it took to retrieve it from the canyons usually made the venture unprofitable.

Railroads made it much easier for Americans to visit the Grand Canyon and neighboring sites such as Famous Antelope Canyon (above)

Instead, some enterprising settlers tried to turn a profit through tourism. The voyages of Powell and others still captured the imaginations of the public, and railroad transportation allowed citizens of any age and fitness level to experience some of the wonders of the Grand Canyon without having to endure the hardships. Visitors didn't need to trudge down into the canyons but could enjoy the scenery from the

southern high ground, known as the South Rim. Stagecoaches would bring tourists from the railroads to the South Rim, where settlers operated simple lodges.

Among these early visitors was Indiana senator Benjamin Harrison, who proposed legislation in Congress several times from 1882 to 1886 to create a Grand Canyon National Park. All of his proposals failed, but when Harrison became president, he established the Grand Canyon Forest Reserve in 1893, even though much of the land contained little forest. The reserve designation encompassed a huge area but was less restrictive than a national park. Existing residents and businesses were allowed to remain within the region, but further land claims were limited. Ranchers and miners were not happy with the regulations, but they were far outnumbered by people who voiced a desire for even greater protection for the Grand Canyon. In the mid-1890s, a stretch of railroad was completed that led directly to the South Rim, boosting tourism. This, in turn, increased business for local settlers, the Santa Fe railroad company, and nearby Arizona railroad towns such as Flagstaff and Williams.

President Harrison's successor, Theodore Roosevelt, visited the Grand Canyon in 1903, and the well-traveled outdoorsman called it the most impressive scenery he'd ever seen. In 1906, Roosevelt created the Grand Canyon Game Reserve, which did little more than ban hunting in the already existing forest reserve. Two years later, he created the Grand Canyon National Monument. Still within the confines of the forest reserve, the monument was managed by the U.S. Forest Service.

For the Grand Canyon to become a national park, it would need the approval of Congress, but bills introduced in 1910 and 1911 were defeated. Part of the problem was that Arizona was only a **territory**

During his four years as president, Benjamin Harrison gave protection to the Grand Canyon and saw six states join the U.S.

and had no representation in Congress to fight for the cause. In 1912, Arizona gained statehood. By then, it was becoming evident that the Grand Canyon could not function well as a national forest, a wildlife reserve, and a monument—all at the same time, yet with different boundaries—under the direction of an organization intended for only forest management.

In 1919, Arizona politicians introduced new legislation to make the Grand Canyon a national park. The bill was passed, and on February 26, the Grand Canyon National Park Act was signed by president Woodrow Wilson. The park encompassed 1,279 square miles (3,313 sq km) in northern Arizona along the Colorado River and was put under the control of the NPS. Grand Canyon National Park received 44,000 visitors during its first year of operation. After going largely unappreciated for centuries, it seemed the true splendor of the Grand Canyon was finally being realized.

Stagecoaches, the first convenient way for the average traveler to reach the canyon, remain a symbol of the American West

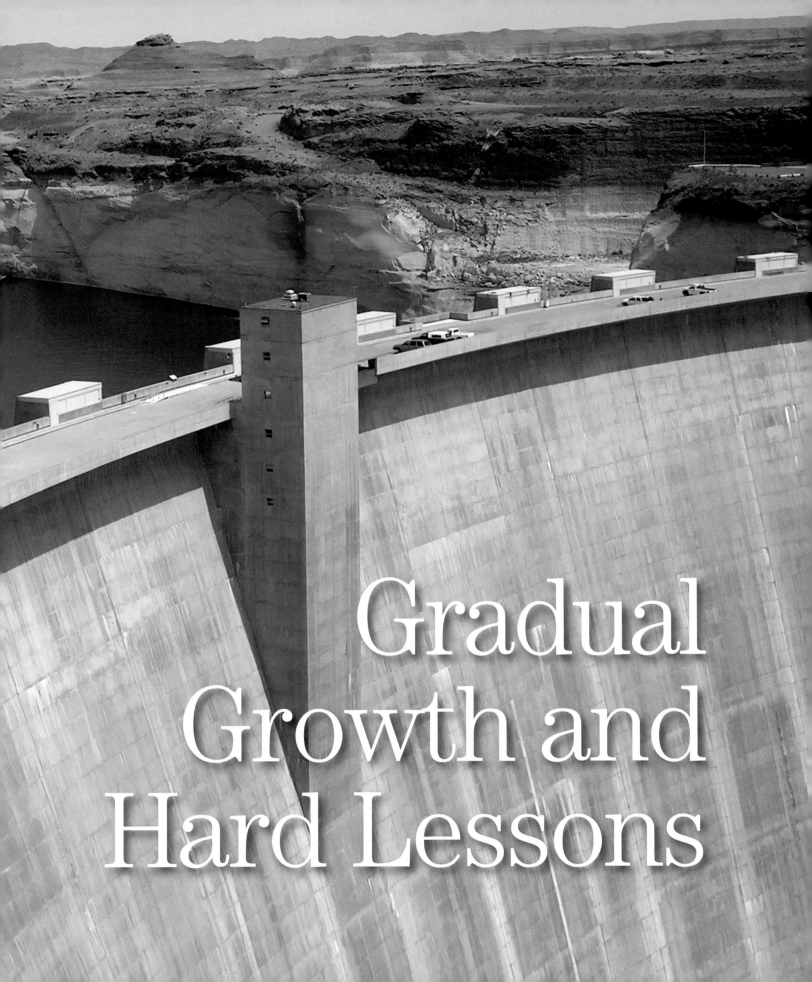

Gradual
Growth and
Hard Lessons

Hunting, now banned in the park, played a major role in reshaping the Grand Canyon's animal populations in the early 1900s

Before, during, and after the Grand Canyon's establishment as a national park, the region underwent many changes that affected the land itself, the ecosystems it contained, and the tourist experience of the place. In almost every case, these changes occurred as a direct result of human actions, sometimes with unintended consequences.

When the Grand Canyon Game Reserve was created by President Roosevelt in 1906, it needed someone to manage the wildlife within it. The man chosen for the job was James "Uncle Jim" Owens. As a boy, Owens had worked as a cowhand for famous cattleman Charles Goodnight, and as a young man, he had earned a reputation as an outstanding animal handler, hunter, and outdoorsman. Owens's duty as the Grand Canyon's game warden was to protect game animals—specifically deer—in the reserve. This involved mostly two steps: banning deer hunting and killing predators that fed upon deer. Owens hunted and guided hunts along the Grand Canyon's North Rim, where wildlife was most abundant. During his tenure, he claimed to have killed more than 500 mountain lions, and he assisted other hunters and trappers in the killing of hundreds more mountain lions, bobcats, and coyotes. Even President Roosevelt went on one such mountain lion hunt in 1913. The aging Owens resigned from the warden position after 12 years, but predator hunting continued, even after the Grand Canyon became a national park.

The plan to protect deer soon backfired. By the 1920s, deer were so overpopulated along the North Rim that thousands starved to death in the winter. Finally recognizing the important role that predators played in maintaining a balanced ecosystem, park officials banned further hunting in 1924. Mountain lion numbers never really recovered, though, and the big cats remain rare in the park to this day.

Fortunately, not all park decisions turned out so poorly. In 1927,

Congress extended the borders of Grand Canyon National Park to include sections of land that were previously part of the Kaibab National Forest, which borders both the South and North rims of the Grand Canyon. This addition increased vital wildlife habitat in the park and better protected the animals within it, as hunting was permitted in the Kaibab National Forest but not in Grand Canyon National Park.

The protected areas of the Grand Canyon region expanded again in 1932, when president Herbert Hoover—using his powers under a law called the Antiquities Act—created a new Grand Canyon National Monument (the original monument of that name had already been incorporated into the national park). The new monument was not officially part of the national park but shared its western border and contained 300 square miles (777 sq km) of land and a 40-mile (64 km) portion of the Colorado River. This addition and the land restrictions it involved did not please many ranchers and landowners in the area, who charged that Hoover used his presidential power to create the monument because he knew Congress wouldn't endorse an expansion of the park.

Recognizable by its large, mulelike ears, the hardy and adaptable mule deer is found throughout much of western America

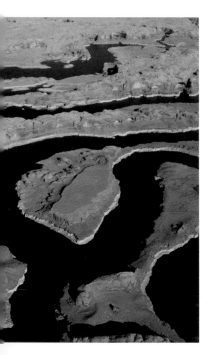

Dramatically restricting water flow, the Glen Canyon Dam created the sprawling Lake Powell (pictured), America's second-largest artificial lake

Dams, too, became a matter of regional contention in the 1930s. In 1936, construction of the massive Hoover Dam was completed on the Colorado River to the west of Grand Canyon National Park. By creating **hydroelectric power** and filling the Lake Mead **reservoir**, the dam provided both electricity and water to parts of California, Nevada, and Arizona. And with the reservoir becoming a popular area for sport fishing, boating, and water skiing, the dam seemed to be a major success. But the drawback, according to critics that included conservationists, was that, by artificially creating a lake and changing the river's flow, natural habitats and ecosystems were harmed. Erosion would change, and plant and animal life both in and out of the water would be affected. Although Hoover Dam and Lake Mead were far downstream from the Grand Canyon, miles of the park's western waterways would flood when the reservoir filled up.

Yet it seemed that the greatest threat to the Grand Canyon was not the Hoover Dam itself but the trend it set in motion. The population of the arid American Southwest was rapidly growing and needed increasing amounts of power and water. The solution was to keep building dams. In 1963, construction of the Glen Canyon Dam was completed. The Glen Canyon Dam, like Hoover Dam, was built on the Colorado River, but this one was upstream of the Grand Canyon. The controlled release of water at the dam changed the natural flow of the river through the park, which in turn altered the buildup and movement of sediment and changed the habitat for plants and animals.

Besides the effect the Glen Canyon Dam was already having on the Grand Canyon, it offered a glimpse of what might happen if a dam were ever built within the park. Glen Canyon had been a remote, sculpted landscape similar to the Grand Canyon. But the dam had flooded the

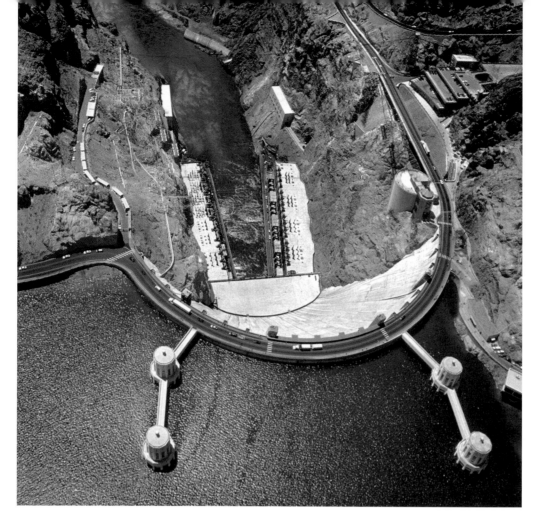

gorge, and the collected water concealed the intricate rock formations and colorful layers of earth that had developed over millions of years. When the Bureau of Reclamation proposed the building of two dams within the Grand Canyon in 1963, conservationists such as David Brower railed against them and soon had the public on their side. The dam proposals were squashed, and the park remains dam-free today.

In 1969, president Lyndon B. Johnson oversaw the creation of Marble Canyon National Monument just upriver from the Grand Canyon and along the northeastern corner of the national park. By 1975, this monument and the one Hoover had created 4 decades earlier were both incorporated into Grand Canyon National Park, finally forming the 1,904-square-mile (4,931 sq km) park that exists today. Twenty-five years later, another monument in the region was created by presidential proclamation when, in 2000, Bill Clinton set aside land for the Grand

The huge Hoover Dam has become a tourist attraction in its own right, and many visitors to the Grand Canyon also take in the dam

Building the Grand Canyon Skywalk was a challenge, as it is in a remote spot about 70 miles (113 km) from the nearest town

Canyon–Parashant National Monument, which is almost as large as the national park and immediately to the north.

A recent controversy within the park involved differing views on how and when Grand Canyon was formed. Scientific explanations based on geological records are more commonly accepted, but many **creationists** believe the entire region was shaped in the last 4,000 years or so and formed rapidly following a great flood as described in the Bible. Beginning in 2003, some literature sold in the park's bookshops described the region and its formation from a creationist point of view, and a dispute arose between people demanding the books be removed from the park and those insisting they remain. Even park officials were not in agreement on the matter, which involved not only a direct science-versus-creation debate but also the issue of tolerance for different beliefs. To quell protests from the scientific community, creationist books were displayed apart from science-based books within Grand Canyon's shops.

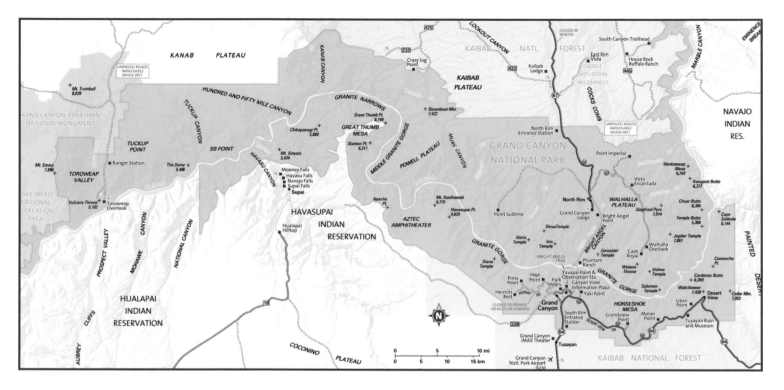

A more highly publicized change to the Grand Canyon experience came about in 2007 with the construction of the Grand Canyon Skywalk. Located just outside the park's border—at a place called Grand Canyon West—and operated by the Hualapai Indian tribe, the Skywalk is a large, horseshoe-shaped platform that extends 70 feet (21 m) beyond a cliff edge 4,000 feet (1,219 m) above the Colorado River. The platform deck and side barriers are made of transparent glass, which offers tourists unique views and a sense of floating in mid-air. The Skywalk was controversial because many people saw the ultra-modern structure and its high admission fee ($30 per person as of 2012) as conflicting with the natural, undisturbed essence of the canyon. Such concerns only increased as construction continued at the site following the Skywalk's completion. As of 2012, plans for the decidedly non-rustic tourist complex included the addition of a movie theater and a high-end bar and restaurant.

Grand Canyon National Park is entirely within Arizona but draws near the borders of both Utah and Nevada

Easy Sightseeing and Extreme Adventure

Grand Canyon National Park receives nearly 5 million visitors per year, making it second in popularity only to the Great Smoky Mountains among America's national parks. A key contributing factor to this high attendance is the park's proximity to the city of Las Vegas, Nevada, as tours of Hoover Dam and the Grand Canyon have become staples of many Vegas visitors' itineraries. Since the Grand Canyon is frequently viewed more as a side trip and less as a primary destination, the average tourist to the Grand Canyon does not spend much time there. In fact, many of the park's visitors do little more than stop at a few scenic overlooks.

In Grand Canyon National Park, road access typically determines where guests go, and the most prominent roads lead to the South Rim and—to a much lesser extent—the North Rim. Both areas sit above the canyon near the eastern edge of the park, and as their names suggest, South Rim is south of the Colorado River, and North Rim is north of the waterway.

From left to right: a view from Mather Point, Yavapai Observation Station, a view from Hopi Point, the historic Grand Canyon Railway Station

The South Rim is where the first railroads brought visitors more than a century ago. The railroad is still there, and the South Rim continues to be the busiest part of the park, with about 90 percent of Grand Canyon's guests stopping there. Grand Canyon Village is the starting point and hub of activity for the South Rim, and it contains the park's largest visitor center as well as shops, hotels, restaurants, and shuttle

bus services. It is from Grand Canyon Village that the most popular sightseeing routes branch out.

The seven-mile (11 km) Hermit Road leads tourists directly to noteworthy attractions including Mather Point, Yavapai Observation Station, Hopi Point, and Hermits Rest. Mather Point is within a short walking distance of the visitor center and may be the most frequently used overlook in the park. Yavapai Observation Station offers various geological exhibits and features a glass-enclosed observation room, making it popular during inclement weather. Hopi Point allows visitors to see for many miles across the canyons below, and its unobstructed views are ideal for both sunrises and sunsets. Hermits Rest is a limestone building constructed in a hillside near the canyon rim. Although it appears rickety, the structure has stood since 1914 and today functions as a gift shop. Thanks to these attractions and several other overlooks and **trailheads**, Hermit Road is heavily traveled. During the park's busiest months (March to November), tourists must use buses, bicycles, or their feet instead of cars on this route.

A longer scenic road that also originates near Grand Canyon Village is Desert View Drive. Covering 23 miles (37 km), this route heads in the opposite direction of Hermit Road and is open to car travel year round. Although Desert View Drive is less popular than Hermit Road, finding parking spaces at the many overlooks along this roadway may be difficult

in the summer. Desert View Drive also leads to various picnic areas and trailheads.

A straight line "as the crow flies" from the South Rim to the North Rim would be only about 10 miles (16 km), but because no roads pass over or through the canyon, driving from rim to rim is a 220-mile (354 km) trip. Only 10 percent of Grand Canyon visitors stop at the North Rim, and with the exception of the historic Grand Canyon Lodge, there is little focus on man-made facilities. Bright Angel Point is to the North Rim what Mather Point is to the South Rim: an easily accessible, classic overlook of the Grand Canyon. Lightly traveled roads lead from the Grand Canyon Lodge to overlooks including Cape Royal and Point Imperial. Cape Royal provides fantastic panoramic views in nearly every

Cape Royal, which is a long ridge of jutting rock, is considered an essential stop by most tourists who visit the North Rim

direction, and Point Imperial—at 8,803 feet (2,683 m)—is the highest point in the park and overlooks the stretch of land where the narrow Marble Canyon dramatically widens to the vast dimensions for which the Grand Canyon is famous.

Aside from having alternative vantage points and fewer amenities, the North Rim differs from the South Rim in other ways. Its average elevation is 1,000 feet (305 m) higher, contributing to cooler, wetter weather, which may be a plus in midsummer but also brings snow that causes North Rim facilities and services to close from mid-October to mid-May. The different elevations and climates also create different ecosystems and forest types. Both rims are bordered by portions of the Kaibab National Forest, which helps promote vibrant wildlife—including mule deer and elk—and scenery around the Grand Canyon's rims.

For tourists who are not content to simply view the canyons from overlooks or through car windows, Grand Canyon National Park offers

The view from lofty Point Imperial is especially spectacular for early risers who are at the overlook in time to watch the sun come up

While Grand Canyon hiking trails can range from very leisurely to potentially dangerous, virtually all lead to some unforgettable sights

a variety of hiking opportunities that begin at both rims. Some of these hikes are really just short walks from parking lots to scenic overlooks. Other trails wind through forests on the upper rims, but the routes that really separate Grand Canyon hiking from that done nearly anywhere else are those leading down into the canyon. Some of these strenuous trails cover about 20 miles (32 km) round trip and may have elevation changes close to a mile (1.6 km).

Park visitors wanting to descend into the canyon and return without exerting themselves too much have the option of taking guided mule rides, and the sturdy animals have safely carried Grand Canyon tourists over steep, narrow paths for more than a century. Among the mule rides offered at the South Rim are one-day or overnight camping treks that descend 3,500 feet (1,067 m). Novice riders should be aware that these rides may cause sore muscles and backsides and can be nerve-racking for people with any fear of heights. Fortunately, both of the upper rims offer shorter rides across flatter terrain that is suitable for most riders.

*The mules used
to carry riders into
the canyon are big,
well-trained, and
safe; in more than a
century, no tourist
has ever died on
the venture*

While rafting down the Colorado River offers plenty of thrills, it also provides calmer moments in which to enjoy the scenery

The longer South Rim mule rides may be booked solid a year in advance, so reservations are a must.

The Colorado River at the bottom of the Grand Canyon is accessible only by trail or boat, but the recreation and sights the river provide are well worth the trip for many guests. Whitewater rafting is hugely popular in the park, and outfitters offer adventures ranging widely in time commitment and difficulty. Trips may take less than a day or last a few weeks and involve campouts on the riverbanks. Visitors may pay for guided services provided in the park or apply for a permit to raft on their own. Either way, tourists need to make plans well in advance, as a limited number of trips and permits are available.

Guests staying overnight in Grand Canyon National Park will find most of the lodging and camping options near the South Rim. The six hotels include the El Tovar Hotel, which was built in 1905 and—despite its rustic décor—offers the most luxurious accommodations in the park, not to mention outstanding views from its clifftop location. Phantom Ranch is located on the canyon floor and can be reached only by foot or mule.

Grand Canyon Lodge, on the North Rim, may be the most impressive building in the park with its stone and wood construction and expansive, cathedral-like main hall.

Three campgrounds are on the South Rim, two are on the canyon floor, and one is on the North Rim. Only Trailer Village (South Rim) offers RV hookups, and only the Mather (South Rim) and North Rim campgrounds have showers nearby. Reservations are recommended for these three campgrounds, and the two campgrounds within the canyon require **backcountry** permits.

Whether guests have a lot of time or a little, are interested in popular attractions or seclusion, or seek rigorous activity or mere samples of the park's recreational offerings, the Grand Canyon can meet their needs. As it always has been, the worth of Grand Canyon is whatever people determine it to be, and for almost a century, visitors have considered Grand Canyon National Park to be one of the most awe-inspiring spectacles on the planet.

From gazing across miles of empty space to mounting a sure-footed mule, the Grand Canyon has something for every visitor

Animals

Soaring Symbol of Hope

California condors nearly went extinct in the 1980s due to habitat loss and poaching. Through careful recovery and reintroduction programs, about 200 of these enormous birds now live in a few wild habitats, including the Grand Canyon. Condors belong to the New World vulture family, and with their bare, fleshy heads, they may be considered ugly when viewed up-close. However, they are truly impressive creatures when seen soaring high above the earth at speeds approaching 50 miles (80 km) per hour. With wingspans of close to 10 feet (3 m), California condors are the largest land birds in North America. While in flight, condors can be distinguished from similar-looking turkey vultures by the white markings under their wings.

Canyon Cliff Dwellers

*Rattlesnakes' preferred habitats are dry, rocky crevices. This makes the Grand Canyon a paradise for rattlesnakes, and the national park contains six species of the venomous reptiles, including the **endemic** Grand Canyon rattlesnake. All species have the distinctive rattles on their tails, which may be shaken as a warning when the snakes feel*

threatened. "Rattlers" range in length from two to five feet (.6–1.5 m) and kill rodents, lizards, and birds by injecting them with venom and then swallowing them whole. Rattlesnakes do not deliberately pursue humans but may strike if people get too close.

On Foot the Easy Way

Hermit Road on the South Rim is one of the most commonly traveled stretches in Grand Canyon National Park. Running near Hermit Road but even closer to the edge of the canyon is the Rim Trail. This gradually sloping, mostly paved hiking trail passes the same historic buildings and famous overlooks as Hermit Road but allows guests to stretch their legs a little and experience views of the canyon that can't be had from the road turn-offs. Walkers can easily hop on or off the free shuttle buses wherever Hermit Road and Rim Trail meet, making this trail inviting, even for reluctant hikers.

A Quiet Retreat

Grand Canyon visitors who want to get away from crowds, get out of their cars, and experience varied scenery—all without grueling activity—might consider the Widforss Trail on the North Rim. This

hike covers 10 miles (16 km) round trip but is easy walking, and the elevation changes only about 400 feet (122 m) during the trek. The trail alternates between canyon views and paths among forests and wildflowers. Near the end of the hike is a picnic area and the Widforss Point overlook: a dramatic conclusion to the low-traffic trail. This day hike may be completed in about six hours, but backcountry camping in the area is also an option.

Ancient Life Preserved

Several national parks, including Zion and Bryce Canyon, are just north of Grand Canyon and are part of the same Colorado Plateau Province. However, Grand Canyon tourists wanting a change of pace might instead visit Petrified Forest National Park, which is in eastern Arizona and about a four-hour drive from the South Rim. While there aren't really forests of petrified trees, visitors can see fossilized trunks, branches, and stumps that are up to 200 million years old. The same climate and terrain that preserved this plant material also preserved animal bones, and the park displays fossils from dinosaurs and other animals of the region from ages past.

Grand Canyon's "Young" Neighbor

Many people associate earth-shaping volcanoes with prehistoric times. However, just a two-hour drive southeast of Grand Canyon's South Rim lies Sunset Crater Volcano National Monument, which features a volcanic **cinder cone** *that was formed almost 1,000 years ago. Even with its bowl-shaped crater, or center, the cone rises 1,120 feet (341 m) above the surrounding landscape, and its peak is 8,042 feet (2,451 m) above sea level. Thanks to its young age, Sunset Crater shows little wear from erosion, and its slopes of hardened lava show fairly early stages of takeover by vegetation. The volcano has now been dormant, or inactive, for centuries.*

Hiking Smart

Park officials say that hiking to the floor of the Grand Canyon and back in one day is more physically demanding than running a marathon, which is 26.2 miles (42.2 km). Hikers who descend into the canyon should camp a night or two before attempting the climb back up. Day hikers sometimes forget that, in canyon hiking, the hardest part comes last, and they descend too far into the canyon. A good rule is to determine an amount of time one intends to hike, and when a third of that time has passed, turn around and head back up. All hikers should be prepared for extreme midday heat in the lower canyon as well as cold evening temperatures at higher elevations.

Intimidating a Lion

Although mountain lions are rarely seen by Grand Canyon visitors, the big cats—which can grow up to 200 pounds (91 kg)—may occasionally view people as prey, particularly if a person is small and alone. Visitors hiking along the North Rim should travel in groups and keep small children close. In an encounter with a mountain lion, people should not run but instead face the animal, make eye contact, and speak loudly. Extending one's arms or opening a jacket as a means of appearing larger can deter mountain lions, as can throwing branches or other objects within reach while standing tall. In the unlikely event of an attack, fighting back with any available object or even punches and kicks may be enough to turn the cat away.

Glossary

arid: lacking enough water for things to grow; dry and barren

backcountry: an area that is away from developed or populated areas

cinder cone: a cone-shaped formation resulting from the buildup and cooling of molten rock on Earth's surface

creationists: people who believe Earth and all life upon it was created directly by God as literally described in the Bible

ecosystems: communities of animals, plants, and other living things interacting together within an environment

endemic: native and limited to a particular country or region

eroded: worn away by the action of natural forces such as water, wind, or ice

hydroelectric power: electricity produced when water movement turns turbines connected to generators

ice age: a period in Earth's history when temperatures were much colder and glaciers covered much of the planet

plateau: an area of high ground with a fairly level surface

reservoir: a natural or artificial lake or pond in which water is collected and stored for use

territory: an area of the U.S. that falls under control of the American government but does not have the classification of a state

trailheads: the beginning points of walking or hiking trails

tributaries: streams or rivers that connect to a larger river

Selected Bibliography

Arizona & The Grand Canyon. New York: DK Publishing, 2010.

Arizona and the Grand Canyon. New York: Fodor's Travel Publications, 2010.

Christensen, Shane, et al. *National Parks of the American West*. New York: Wiley Publishing, 2010.

Kaiser, James. *Grand Canyon: The Complete Guide.* Ringgold, Ga.: Destination Press, 2007.

National Geographic Guide to the National Parks of the United States. Washington, D.C.: National Geographic Society, 2009.

Schullery, Paul. *America's National Parks: The Spectacular Forces That Shaped Our Treasured Lands*. New York: DK Publishing, 2001.

White, Mel. *Complete National Parks of the United States*. Washington, D.C.: National Geographic Society, 2009.

Websites

Grand Canyon National Park
http://www.nps.gov/grca/index.htm
The official National Park Service site for the Grand Canyon is the most complete online source for information on the park and includes many images and podcasts.

National Geographic: Grand Canyon National Park
http://travel.nationalgeographic.com/travel/national-parks/grand-canyon-national-park/
This site provides a concise visitor's guide to the Grand Canyon, complete with maps, photos, sightseeing suggestions, and links to other popular national parks.

Index